The Journey Along The Way

Raja's Insights

Also by Raja Williams

Imprints In The Sand

www.amazon.com

The Journey Along The Way

Raja's Insights

Raja Williams

The Journey Along The Way Copyright ©2013, 2020: Raja Williams All rights reserved. Printed in the United States of America. No part of this book may be used or reproduced in any manner whatsoever without written permission except in the case of reprints in the context of reviews. This Collection is protected under U.S. and International Copyright laws.

CTU
Publishing Group

a division of Creative Talents Unleashed

www.Rajasinsight.com
www.creativetalentsunleashed.com

2nd Edition

ISBN: 978-1-945791-69-7

Book Description: Brenda-Lee Ranta
Cover Design: Raja Williams
Photos: Pixabay.com
Editor: J. Williams

Dedication

I dedicate this book of insights to all of you that I have had the honor to be in this journey with and to those of you in the future that will come into my journey.

Foreword

Within the confines of our allotted time, each of us are quietly called to go within ourselves; seeking and searching until we finally learn to love all that we are.

Raja Williams has poetically crafted her story of a spiritual journey, while bound in a mortal body. Within the demands of her life: the children, the bills and the job; she discovered tools to go beyond the 'grind' that defines this human experience. Raja takes us on her personal sojourn of inner knowing and soul prodding that caused her to make life changing decisions.

She exquisitely describes the paradox of her egoic struggle with her ability to go within and seek out her personal truth. She speaks of desire for abiding love and companionship, her loss of a sacred relationship, while acquiescing to the truth; that divine timing is both the clay and the sculptor.

Her words are steeped in spirituality, self-discovery and her profound journey to meeting life head-on, with both its joys and heartbreaks. She views each new morning as the opportunity to live within each moment, trusting her inner voice to propel her onward.

"The Journey Along the Way" is a lovely tapestry of words, woven together by a woman seeking her own divine purpose; just as we all are.

Brenda-Lee Ranta, Author

Preface

It's so easy to coast through life in the simplicity or hardships of the journey that we are currently living in. Day after day waking up only to repeat the day before. Wake up, eat, get dressed, go to school or work, come home, eat, relax, and then go to bed just to get up and do the same or some other similar scenario again tomorrow.

This is what we have come to call "living." The question is are you living the life that you would like to live?

In 2006 my journey was suddenly awakened when I finally said "Enough" and decided that I was ready to seek a better way of living. I was tired of feeling alone and *"Stuck"*; stuck on repeating struggles day after day. At the time I did not understand or comprehend that my thinking patterns allowed me to remain stuck.

And so began my search . . .

I was drawn by the vibration of the Spiritual Enrichment Center in Northern California and knew after my very first time attending a Service I was home. It was here I was given spiritual tools to transform my personal life. I spent the next several years learning to discover peace of mind, healing, and inspiration. It is here that I learned the power of our thoughts made manifest. It is true, what we think, takes shape.

We create our lives.

In the spring of 2011, I took a trip down memory lane by booking a weekend getaway in my hometown Irvine, California. I drove from Northern California to Southern California alone. It was the first time I had been to my hometown since I left in 1986. I viewed the home I grew up in, schools, favorite spots, and even went to the beach. It was a lovely getaway and reminder of my youth.

My short getaway went by quick and I packed so many memories of my childhood and growing up into just a few short days. My ten-hour drive home seemed more somber then the journey down which was filled with excitement. I noticed the closer I got to home, the more I felt like I was not "really" going home. I was shocked by these intense feelings! I loved where I lived. My freeway exit to home was coming up. As I was exiting the freeway I suddenly said out loud …

"Where am I suppose to be?" and believe it or not what I heard is *"If you stay here, you will only get more of the same."*

My response to that was, *"I don't think so! I have worked way too hard on bettering my life to continue to accept more of the same."*

Three days later I announced that in three months we were moving to Southern California. My family and friends were shocked and did not know how I could pull off such a task alone with five kids.

In short, I have shared the journey with you of how I found myself by connecting spiritually and following my intuition and creating the life I want. Here I am, living where I was drawn intuitively to live. I am residing in the Southern California, High Desert. Living in the flow of my highest good has brought positive change for my family and I. As well, as brought the right people into my journey at the right times.

From a young age I had thought I would some day publish a book. It was placed right there on that bucket list. You know, that get to someday list. We all have them. Anyway, I was writing and dreaming great stories in my head, but they did not make paper for over twenty years.

I was my only audience.

Then one day my inspirations regarding writing were matched and fueled with a new friend making way into my life's journey. He was not only a prolific published poet, he's also a songwriter, and record producer He shared his work with me regularly, and then called upon me to do the same. *"Read me what you wrote today."* He'd say. He held me accountable even if I just cited noted pages of ideas in the beginning. But soon my poetry came to life and is now pressed upon these pages in *"The Journey Along The Way"*.

And so, my story comes to life through this ink and these words. These are my thoughts. I am honored to share them with you. I only ask that you, "Be Open" while reading my thoughts. Sometimes, through reading and feeling something different you may shift a perception or perspective.

Leaving you to ponder . . .

Please join me on, "*The Journey Along the Way*"

Table of Contents

Breaking Dawn	1
In this Moment	2
Awareness	3
God's Breath	4
This Day is Done	5
Essence of the Trees	6
Emerging into the Light	7
Birth of a Seedling	8
Reflection	9
Who We Are	10
Be Still	11
Illumination	12
Godly Moments	13
Tomorrow's Song	14
The Animal in Me	15
Universal Presence of Love	17
Self – Discovery	18

Let Me Go	19
Holistic Healing	20
Namaste	21
Frequency	22
Freedom of the Butterfly	23
Changing Times	24
Forever Falling	25
Inward Journey	26
It Only Takes One	27
Vrakasana ~ Balance	28
New Stance	29
The Grind	30
Unmasking	31
Breaking Away	33
When I Die	34
Intimate Moments	35
Remembering You	36
In Tune	38
In the Moment	39

Loves Absence	40
Chasing the Sun	41
Surrender	42
Baggage	43
About the Author	44

May the discoveries in the pages that follow inspire you to connect with nature, experience light, and remember the positive in the sometimes negative.

Raja

Raja Williams

Breaking Dawn

Silently she creeps in
Moment by moment
Until the desert land is bathed in her light

A new day has broke in
Birds break into song
Honoring the freedom of today

I inhale this moment as new
Where I am one with you

In silence I sit and pray
experiencing the light
of a brand new day

Raja Williams

In this Moment

Just for a moment
I let it all go
Releasing my worries
And troubles from the past
Inhaling fresh air
A new time at last

Just for a moment
I let it all go
Stopping the stories
I make in my head
Exhaling each breath
As I let go of the past

Just for a moment
I let it all go
Closing my eyes
And releasing the hurt
Knowing this is therapeutically cured

Just for a moment
I let it all go
Having learned
To release the past
And embrace the now

I live *in this moment* with peace from the past.

Raja Williams

Awareness

I am the sound of the wind
Blowing gently through the trees
I am the light that shines
From the sky above
Just as I am in your thoughts
Apart of every act
Every gesture
And Feeling
I am awareness
And this is what it means
To be fully present here
In the now
I am the truth
I am always here
Always moving
And always living
I am what you choose to notice
What you choose to see
And what you hear and think
I am awareness…

The fundamental force that creates self-change

Raja Williams

God's Breath

With the rise and fall of every breath
I become centered

The wind around each heartbeat
Draws me close . . .

Feeling Gods presence
Within each and every breath

His breath becomes mine
His light fills me . . .

The gift of God is within me
The pouring of divine light

I listen in Silence
There is no sound

The stillness of God …

Is quite profound

Raja Williams

This Day is Done

I love this time of day
When she goes down
Moment by moment
Changing in front of your eyes

The hues of reds and oranges
Become softer
Second by second
Until they have faded
Completely into darkness....

This day is done.

 And I give great thanks to the Sun.

Raja Williams

Essence of the Trees

The breeze today
Played a beautiful melody
The sweet sound of the wind
Rustled in the leaves

I find myself with closed eyes
Standing in front of a tree
Taking in the sounds of nature
And all that encompasses me

Bathing in the warmth of the sun
That shines upon my face
Enjoying the day's breeze
Feeling the winds gentle trace

And in the quiet of this moment
Connected internally
I can feel the goddess wisdom
Of this all-mighty tree

No longer standing big and tall
She has fallen to her knees
As she sings the perfect melody…

This song is for the trees.

Raja Williams

Emerging into the Light

I climb from the depths of the mud
My hardships and difficulties unseen
Rising up from below
Breaking through this barrier
Transforming into the light
Unfolding my beauty
Blossoming enlightenment
I am the lotus flower and the lotus flower is me

Raja Williams

Birth of a Seedling

Holes dug
Seeds laid
Ground filled
Water drops fall

Wait
Hope
Love
See

Life sprouts
Roots spread
Stock rising
Breaking through . . .

Into the light

Raja Williams

Reflection

Enjoying the gentle push
of Fall's breathe on my back
and flowing through my hair

Capturing hues of reds and yellows
turned to burnt orange
through the perception of my eyes *reflection*

I am one with the sunset
her warm touch of blissful heat
Radiating from above is felt upon my skin

I have become alive
Drifting away . . .
Into natures bliss

Standing on Earth's holiness
A captured moment I will cherish
I am one with the sunset.

Raja Williams

Who We Are

I have searched deep within me
Diving deep into the soul
An inner knowingness of truth unfolds
Drawing me closer than before

Vibrating with divine energy
The essence of *who we are*
Enlightenment our birthright
Showing us exactly as we are

Past lives are all released
Washing away their karmic debris
Accumulated in the journey
In the history of "me."

I feel immense peace
A sense of healing taking place
I am free at last
From my past

I am now walking in the Light

Raja Williams

Be Still

In the silence
Hear me
Hear the wind
In the sway of the trees

In the silence
Smell me
Blowing in the wind
The scent of a new day in the air

In the silence
Feel me
As your feet stand upon my ground

We are connected as one…
                      Be still in the silence.

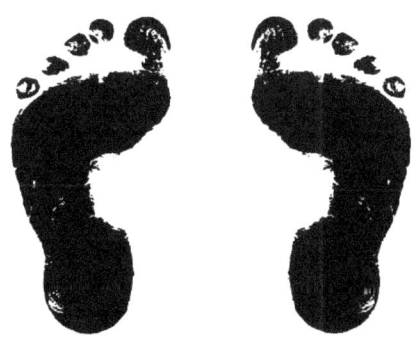

Raja Williams

Illumination

Rays of light
Castaway darkness
Shadows departing
As light penetrates the soul

Illusions fall away
To heightened consciousness
Remembering my birth design

. . . I am the light

Illumination my birthright

Raja Williams

Godly Moments

Just for a moment,
Connect with spirit
And let your soul be fed

Just for a moment,
See with new eyes
And experience life for the gift it is

Just for a moment,
Feel the love and light
Shining upon you

In these moments, we are one.

Raja Williams

Tomorrow's Song

As twilight begins
The birds frolic in the air
One last time

They take flight
And dance across the sky

Singing the melody it will
soon be the night

They swoop
Circle and glide
In the last of today's light

The sun gently sets
One by one they fly to
their nests
And there is no more light

The dusk is here
To bid the birds goodnight

Until tomorrow's new light
We say goodnight, and look forward to the
Birds awakening to tomorrow's song.

Raja Williams

The Animal in Me

I am mighty like the elephant
All obstacles I overcome
Moving forward in my destiny
Achievements easily won

I am as graceful as the whale
Swimming in divine loves bath
Encouraging communication
Along my soul's gentle path

I am resilient like the horse
Agility steadfast
Compromise my freedom
I will take off running fast

I am fertile as the rabbit
Reproduction happens fast
Unique manifestations
Keeps imagination moving fast

I am strong like the bear
Standing my ground
Solitude ingests me
Leaving protection my surround

I am swift like the fox

Raja Williams

Using life skills I have learned
Rigid thinking patterns adjourned
Flexibility the continuum of how I learn

Encompassing the animal spirit
As we are both one and the same
Living life on this journey
Great spirits of this plane.

Raja Williams

Universal Presence of Love

Rays of light spiral
Like beams from the sun
Sharing my heart presence
As we become one

As you awaken
You see the window to the soul
An ocean of love
A vibration call

Amplified feelings
Harmonized with love
Sensing the aliveness
The divine substance of love

Pulling back the veil
Remembering who you are
A divine being of light
A bright shining star

Connected in your heart center
Moved by the light
Your sense of soul love
Having just taken flight

Raja Williams

Self - Discovery

Searching for purpose in my life agreements

Expecting great things to unfold along the journey

Lessons learned each and every day

Faith holding my hand each and every step of the way

Day in and day out I find reasons to be in love with life

I couldn't imagine life any other way

Surrounding myself with positive influence

Cause that's the only way to live

Opening my mind to new perspectives

Vowing to live a life that remains consistent both

Externally and internally and always

Remembering my blessings while

Yearning to be the best me along the way. . .

I journey in *self-discovery* each and every day.

Raja Williams

Let Me Go

Confined by my inability to see and experience change
Cowering in my own self-doubts and fears

Shackled to false beliefs and misinformation

Chained to societies misconceptions

Until I say . . . "Enough!"

Unbind me and set me free

Let me soar in my own ideas and thoughts

May new perceptions be seen and appreciated

Embracing change and transformation

I am free!

Raja Williams

Holistic Healing

I arose with the morning sun
Ready to experience the land
Take its first early morning breath
Crisp invigorating fresh air
Birds singing to one another
The hum of gnats can be heard
I walk in silence
Following the dirt trail
Prepared to release and let go
In the meadow ahead
I can see the hot springs
Steam slowly lifting above the water
As I approach the Meditation Pool
I am clear in my thoughts and intentions
I enter the space holding gratitude
My clothes are shed
I go into the pool naked
Ready to receive this healing
The water soothing and warm
My feet grounded in the soft sand
Nature and me hand in hand
I close my eyes and go into reflection
Feeling the waters healing intentions

I relax and let go…

Raja Williams

Namaste

Happiness penetrates my soul
when I catch glimpse of you

Senses vividly awakened and immersed in light
I am lost in the visions of joy that dance in my head

Together we celebrate and honor our life on this earth
A splendid rendition of a midsummer's day

At this moment I bow to you and say . . .

"Namaste."

* Meaning of Namaste: "I honor the place within you where the entire Universe dwells. I honor the place within you, which is of love, of truth, of light, and of peace. When you are in that place in you, and I am in that place in me, we are one."

Raja Williams

Frequency

We all want to get there
To that higher place
Close your eyes and concentrate
Forgetting time and space

Feel that energy
As you start to gravitate
Rising in awareness
You'll reach a heightened state

Shifting your consciousnes
Divine energy received
To live this life with nothing but
Peace and harmony

So I take this time . . .

Each and every day
To get my mind connected
With a higher *frequency*

Raja Williams

Freedom of the Butterfly

Life begins…
For twenty-one days
I eat and grow

Trusting the process…
I rest for twenty-one days
And then I awaken

Having Transformed…
I am different
Time has past

Embracing the change…
My wings start to flutter
I let go

And I fly, fly, fly

Raja Williams

Changing Times

The winds of change have blown my way
Circulating like a quiet storm ready to break
Swirling in emotions past and present
How you feel becomes most relevant

I could simply fear change and deny it to
Sticking to yesterday's visions that I hold to be true
Or embrace what new comes this way

Change can be scary, this we know
It's hard to release the patterns that we hold to be true
But truth be told …

Change is the only constant in life that can't be controlled
So it's time to change the way we think
Embracing changes as they come

Living the moments one by one.

Raja Williams

Forever Falling

As sands of time pass through the hourglass . . .

One by one falling in a new direction

Fear released in the moment of the fall

Freedom felt in the fall

Revelations realized through the fall

Falling, falling, falling . . .

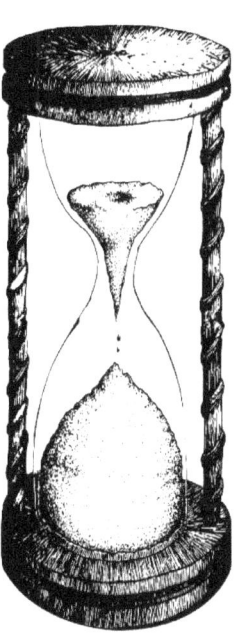

Forever eternally in the freedom of the fall.

Raja Williams

Inward Journey

Listening to my body talk to me. . .

Hunger
       Thirst
              Fatigue
                      Stress
                              Pleasure . . .

All major signs in which our bodies speak to us.
But there are also subtle messages from our bodies as well

Discomfort
          Unease
                    Peacefulness
                              Relaxation . . .

Are you turning inward and listening to yourself?

Quieting down the outer chatter
To attend to your inner self.

Listen inwardly. . .Suspending all judgments. Not blocking what you may be hearing, but accepting it as it is. Connect more deeply with yourself. Go on an inward journey and expand life itself, welcoming the inward journey as an extension of one's self.

Raja Williams

It Only Takes One

It only takes One
To enter and pass-through
Into a higher perspective
To find the positive,
In the sometimes negative
To have the will
To live in the now
Through these difficult
Trying times we feel
Learning to only allow
Exemplified power of good
To control this reality
It only takes One
To know that fear
Is natural,
But it does not have
To control us
It only takes One
To understand that
We objectify our thoughts,
What we think about
Is what we get more of
And we must understand
That it is up to us
To stomp out negativity.

Together in unity, we are the Power of One

Raja Williams

Vrakasana ~

BalanceFirmly rooted in the soil of the earth

Strong instance as I stand tall

Flexible to the winds gentle push

Aligned with the power of balance

I am Vrksa ~ Tree

(Yoga Pose: Tree Posture)

Raja Williams

New Stance

Rejection brings the

Experience of coldness

Jutting great pain yet

Enables freedom and

Change to take place

Taking us in a new direction, our

Inner voice is awakened

Old disappointments released…

Now at this moment

I let go of the past, rejection giving me a new stance at last.

Raja Williams

The Grind

Feelings of discouragement creeping in from the daily grind

Restless mind finding all the faults I normally don't see

Unfavorable outcome currently in my perception
Satisfactory agreements must be made among us
Trading hours for dollars to make me self sufficient
Resentfully being underpaid . . . Minimum wage

A robot made to carry out superior's orders

Time counting from the punch in to punch out
Employed . . . is what it says on paper
Disappointed is how I feel today

Thank God tomorrow's a brand new day.

Raja Williams

Unmasking

Each and every day
When I step into the world I put my smile on
I wear my happy face
For everyone to see
And they believe it's really me

I smile at complete strangers
And laugh at silly jokes
Appearing full of life….
But underneath the smoke
I really am a joke
Wearing this mask
Having no hope

When I am home alone
I am isolated and lonely
My face shows
A completely different story

But with tomorrow's new light
I will wake again
Putting on my happy mask
And pretending to be, not who I am
Sometimes I wonder…
Will happiness rub off on me?
Because I wear them more than
The unhappy me.

Raja Williams

Maybe when I muster hope
Something different will unfold
Until then, I dig deep in me
Releasing the happy version for all to see
Waiting for the unmasking, of who I am meant to be.

Raja Williams

Breaking Away

Fictional pieces
I have witnessed your faults
Deceptive fragments
You soon shall fall
Hammer in one hand
Chisel in the other
Cracking
Breaking
The mold of me
My skin awakened
To this fresh breathe of air
A sense of freedom
I am now aware
Refusing to be molded
To what society thinks
I am breaking away
These restrictive restraints
Piece by piece
You break
And fall
Giving thanks to my new call
I am clear on my thoughts
And how to proceed
The reality is
I am who I think.

...Shattering the Paradigm of false beliefs

Raja Williams

When I Die

Death becomes
The beauty of life…

As we die for each moment
That we have lived

Feelings become timeless
Immortality achieved

The meaning of death revealed
In each day that we lived

Raja Williams

Intimate Moments

Leveled plains of respect and love
Offer us to step outside of our self-concern.
Vulnerability is not a display of weakness but an
Extension of courage to meet in intimacy.

When I stand in front of you,
I am granted permission to just be me.
Life meeting life through two human hearts.
Life recognizing itself, and the effect is a joyous reunion.

No reference to time because we aren't going anywhere.
Our time is timeless.
The result of two people dwelling together in their hearts.

Learning to allow the healing potential
Existing within my human heart.
Touching you with tenderness

Understanding our "togetherness."
Sharing Human warmth.

Resulting in infinite patience and freedom
Expectations and judgments give wind,
Sexual desires released …
Taking us to the threshold of love.

Love will not let us rest.

Raja Williams

Remembering You

The way you looked at me when we first met
You knew you knew it was me
I saw it in your eyes
The way they danced with joy
and giggled as if, just being gifted as a child.
The sweetness of your smile
and the twinkle of your eyes
made me comfortable
Your company enjoyable
But I did not know it was you
This was something new.
Your words told a different story
One that you found me
And with your mind pulled me in
long before we ever talked
The universe in sync I guess,
Cause here I am!
The more time we spent together
The more I started to feel
Through our shared time,
Conversations, and intimate moments
It was clearly being revealed.

And soon, when I would look at you
You felt as if I was looking through you
As if I could see the future.

Raja Williams

But baby, it was the past
and we found each other at last.
Debris from the past fill you with doubt
You pull away
A crossroad is given and you go astray
Leaving note later….
Goodbye.
And with this, I remember…
Birth is not the start of our timeline.
It is a door through which
an experienced soul enters.
Carrying the baggage and
lessons of past lifetimes.
So I let you go once again
Knowing that we fulfilled
whatever time we were destined
I hold you in my heart,
Until the next life . . .

We depart.

Raja Williams

In Tune

My love is the instrument
that I hold for you.
Deep within you can hear
my sound's vibration call….
Come closer my dear,
and hear each note.
Listen carefully,
as we are in tune.
Come, my love,
and play my song.
Let us hear music together
all night long.

Raja Williams

In the Moment

In moments of silence
I remember your whispers in my ear
Feeling the warmth of your words
Upon the release of your spoken breath
In moments of reflection, I remember your touch
How the rhythm of your hands
Flowed to your poetry whispered in my ear
In moments of pleasure
I remember your feel
Lifting me to a higher vibration
There was no time for poetic contemplation
In the moment
I was free
I let you see the authentic me
The release of my destiny
If only for a moment, you loved me.

Raja Williams

Loves Absence

An experience long forgotten
Caused me to depend on you
For comfort and companionship
To fill the void of loneliness
We become each other's
Sexual pleasures
Separate lives
Busy schedules
Both feeling loves absence
Time goes by…
Feelings are more intense…
Wondering is this love I sense?
In the heat of the moment
I whispered the words
As butterflies wait in suspense
And at that moment
While I wait …

I can only hope that Love becomes my fate

Raja Williams

Chasing the Sun

As the sun is setting
You take my hand
Holding me sweetly in a loving embrace
You lead me to your sacred space
You softly brush my hair from my eyes
As your finger traces my face
Your eyes filled with desire and lust
Loving you is my fate
Your hands move swiftly
As you undress me, exposing only skin
Your sweet kisses blessing my body
My weakness is my sin
Souls intertwined fiery hot
Making Love all night long
In the darkness of his space
I let love enter my sacred place
With Dawn approaching, I must go
Separated by distance and time you know
Thankful for your loving touch
Chasing the sun is today's greatest rush

Surrender

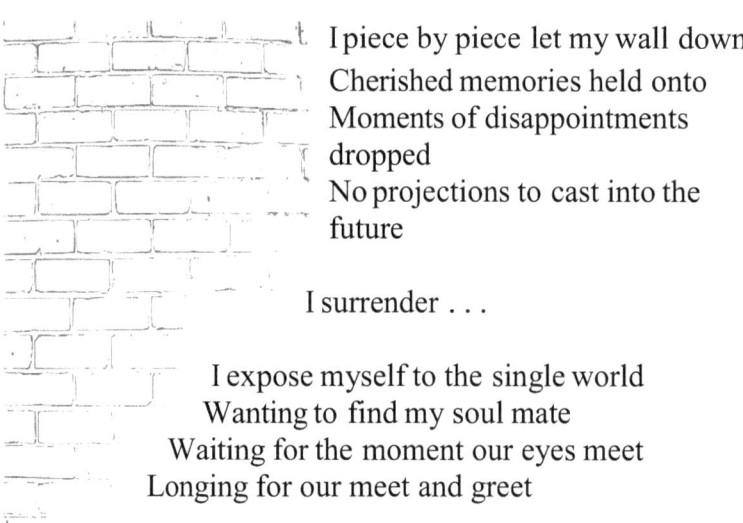

    I piece by piece let my wall down
    Cherished memories held onto
    Moments of disappointments dropped
    No projections to cast into the future

    I surrender . . .

    I expose myself to the single world
    Wanting to find my soul mate
    Waiting for the moment our eyes meet
    Longing for our meet and greet

I surrender . . .

Days turn into nights
As time slips into the future
Where are you, my love?

I await you . . .

Surrendering the feeling of being alone.

Raja Williams

Baggage

I dragged it with me . . .
every
    hurt,
        rejection,
            strain,
and every other fragile moment of disappointment

All of my past heartbreaks brought . . .
fear,
   disappointment,
            pain,
                anxiety,
and all the unhappy endings that go with failed
relationship's

For years I buried all those feelings in. . . .
deep,
    quiet,
        forgotten,
             places
where I learned to forget the feelings and emotions related
to heartbreak

Then suddenly one day you came along . . .
and
   my
      baggage
            is wide OPEN.

About the Author

My name has led me on an interesting journey through life. I am a free-spirited woman that embraces love and light. I was born with a name that in Sanskrit means "King" and in Arabic stands for "Hope". I am an American woman born in the United States of America with an English, Irish, and Finnish ethnic heritage. My name does NOT match my ethnic background, which I believe has helped to define me as a unique being.

I Am Raja

I walk to the beat of my own drum. Following my inner guidance while connecting spiritually. I practice noticing life with new eyes daily. I question my perceptions and I am constantly challenging my thoughts.

www.Rajasinsight.com

www.ingramcontent.com/pod-product-compliance
Lightning Source LLC
Chambersburg PA
CBHW061344040426
42444CB00011B/3074